Animal BFFs

Extraordinary Ties Between Unusual Friends!

★ BY STEPHANIE R. PEARMAIN ★

SCHOLASTIC

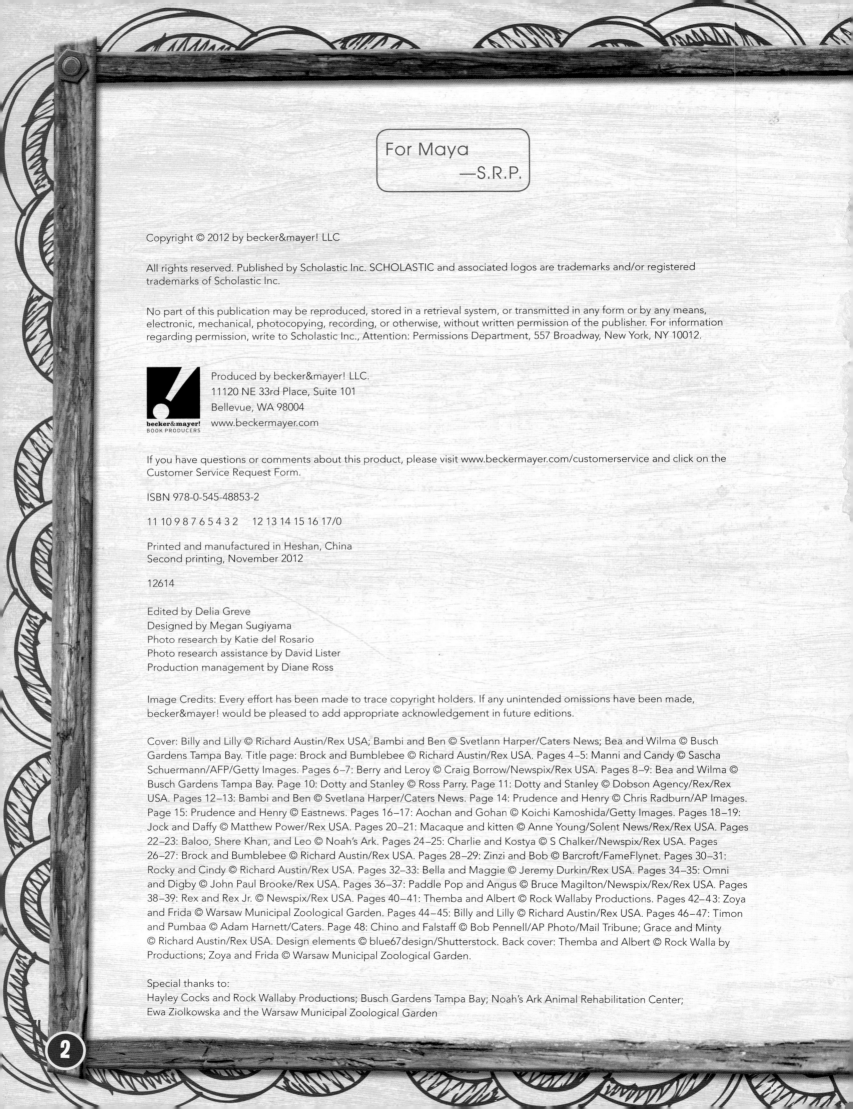

For Maya
—S.R.P.

Produced by becker&mayer! LLC.
11120 NE 33rd Place, Suite 101
Bellevue, WA 98004
www.beckermayer.com

If you have questions or comments about this product, please visit www.beckermayer.com/customerservice and click on the Customer Service Request Form.

ISBN 978-0-545-48853-2

11 10 9 8 7 6 5 4 3 2   12 13 14 15 16 17/0

Printed and manufactured in Heshan, China
Second printing, November 2012

12614

Edited by Delia Greve
Designed by Megan Sugiyama
Photo research by Katie del Rosario
Photo research assistance by David Lister
Production management by Diane Ross

Image Credits: Every effort has been made to trace copyright holders. If any unintended omissions have been made, becker&mayer! would be pleased to add appropriate acknowledgement in future editions.

Cover: Billy and Lilly © Richard Austin/Rex USA; Bambi and Ben © Svetlann Harper/Caters News; Bea and Wilma © Busch Gardens Tampa Bay. Title page: Brock and Bumblebee © Richard Austin/Rex USA. Pages 4–5: Manni and Candy © Sascha Schuermann/AFP/Getty Images. Pages 6–7: Berry and Leroy © Craig Borrow/Newspix/Rex USA. Pages 8–9: Bea and Wilma © Busch Gardens Tampa Bay. Page 10: Dotty and Stanley © Ross Parry. Page 11: Dotty and Stanley © Dobson Agency/Rex/Rex USA. Pages 12–13: Bambi and Ben © Svetlana Harper/Caters News. Page 14: Prudence and Henry © Chris Radburn/AP Images. Page 15: Prudence and Henry © Eastnews. Pages 16–17: Aochan and Gohan © Koichi Kamoshida/Getty Images. Pages 18–19: Jock and Daffy © Matthew Power/Rex USA. Pages 20–21: Macaque and kitten © Anne Young/Solent News/Rex/Rex USA. Pages 22–23: Baloo, Shere Khan, and Leo © Noah's Ark. Pages 24–25: Charlie and Kostya © S Chalker/Newspix/Rex USA. Pages 26–27: Brock and Bumblebee © Richard Austin/Rex USA. Pages 28–29: Zinzi and Bob © Barcroft/FameFlynet. Pages 30–31: Rocky and Cindy © Richard Austin/Rex USA. Pages 32–33: Bella and Maggie © Jeremy Durkin/Rex USA. Pages 34–35: Omni and Digby © John Paul Brooke/Rex USA. Pages 36–37: Paddle Pop and Angus © Bruce Magilton/Newspix/Rex/Rex USA. Pages 38–39: Rex and Rex Jr. © Newspix/Rex USA. Pages 40–41: Themba and Albert © Rock Wallaby Productions. Pages 42–43: Zoya and Frida © Warsaw Municipal Zoological Garden. Pages 44–45: Billy and Lilly © Richard Austin/Rex USA. Pages 46–47: Timon and Pumbaa © Adam Harnett/Caters. Page 48: Chino and Falstaff © Bob Pennell/AP Photo/Mail Tribune; Grace and Minty © Richard Austin/Rex USA. Design elements © blue67design/Shutterstock. Back cover: Themba and Albert © Rock Walla by Productions; Zoya and Frida © Warsaw Municipal Zoological Garden.

Special thanks to:
Hayley Cocks and Rock Wallaby Productions; Busch Gardens Tampa Bay; Noah's Ark Animal Rehabilitation Center; Ewa Ziolkowska and the Warsaw Municipal Zoological Garden

UNLIKELY FRIENDSHIPS AROUND THE WORLD

What do a horse and a Chihuahua have in common? Why does a snake take a liking to a hamster? Or what happens when a foxhound stops hunting foxes, and decides to befriend one instead?

Around the world in places as remote as jungles, as common as countryside farms, or as protected as sanctuaries and zoos, unlikely friendships have blossomed between animals. These friendships are unexpected, and sometimes even defy nature. How these animals become friends and how they interact aren't all that different from the way people do. They play, learn, comfort, help, and even take care of one another.

There are all kinds of friendships. Turn the page to learn about the lives and stories of some incredible animal BFFs. . . .

MANNI & CANDY

★ EHRINGSHAUSEN, GERMANY ★

In southwest Germany, a wild baby boar was found abandoned in a field. The family who found him bottle-fed him back to health, named him Manni, and introduced him to Candy—the family's Jack Russell terrier. The two became friends and now spend their days playing.

These friends love to leap, roll around, and chase each other in the grass. They also like to run and play hide-and-seek among the trees and bushes.

so cute!

Candy has lots of energy, but Manni can keep up with her. At five weeks old, Manni even began trying to bark like Candy!

After all their games, Manni and Candy often nuzzle together for a rest.

BERRY & LEROY

☆ MELBOURNE, AUSTRALIA ☆

Sometimes opposites really do attract—and Berry and Leroy couldn't be more different! Berry is a Chihuahua and stands just seven inches tall. Leroy is a Clydesdale and stands six feet tall. Berry is actually smaller than one of Leroy's hooves! When Berry was rescued, he was brought to the farm where Leroy lived, and Berry quickly became fascinated with the horse.

Berry enjoys standing on Leroy's back! The perch gives him an excellent view, and when he's had enough, he leaps back down to the ground. Leroy is patient with his little friend, and with his playfulness.

The little Chihuahua has heaps of energy. Berry's idea of a good time is running in and out between Leroy's legs and racing along after his pal.

Leroy weighs almost 2,000 pounds—nearly 300 times more than Berry weighs.

These friends have remained close through some tough times. Once, while Berry was playing, Leroy moved backward and accidentally stepped on Berry. Berry was seriously injured, but to everyone's surprise, the next morning the lucky little dog was up and ready to play again!

BEA & WILMA

Busch Gardens' 65-acre Serengeti Plain exhibit is filled with giraffes, zebras, rare rhinos, African elephants, antelopes, and birds—and they all live together. Two of the inhabitants—Bea the giraffe and Wilma the ostrich—formed an unusual friendship. Both animals were born at Busch Gardens, but their friendship began when Bea was three years old and Wilma was ten years old.

Giraffes use their tongues to explore their surroundings—and sometimes their friends! Wilma doesn't seem to mind Bea's curiosity. Bea even uses her tongue to clean and fluff Wilma's feathers.

A giraffe's tongue is black and is 18–20 inches long!

Bea and Wilma like to stroll around. They are frequently seen resting together by the lake.

BFFs

DOTTY & STANLEY

☆ THROXENBY, ENGLAND ☆

This unlikely pair of friends started as stable mates. Dotty the donkey was found abandoned on the roadside, and Stanley the sheep was orphaned as a newborn. They were both brought to Row Brow Farm. Dotty and Stanley lived together for five years before their friendship blossomed.

A frightening dog attack on Stanley brought Dotty to his rescue. Dotty charged, forcing the dog to let go of Stanley. She then chased the dog off the farm and returned to take care of Stanley.

BFF

The rescue started a true bond between them. Dotty and Stanley spend their days by each other's side.

The People's Dispensary for Sick Animals (PDSA) is an animal charity in England.

Dotty received an award for her heroic act. She was given a Certificate for Animal Bravery from the PDSA. Afterward, Dotty continued to be a protective best friend and to watch over Stanley!

BAMBI & BEN

☆ TROY, MONTANA ☆

The story of an orphaned fawn named Bambi that befriends a fluffy gray rabbit named Thumper is a beloved tale. In 2011, the story got a new twist. A one-day-old fawn was found abandoned. He was rescued and nursed back to health. When he was strong enough, Bambi began meeting other animals. He instantly bonded with none other than Ben, a gray rabbit.

These two cuddly animals love to nap together in the grass.

A fawn is a baby deer.

Bambi and Ben stick together. Bambi hangs out with other animals, but it's never long before he goes looking for Ben.

FRIENDS FOREVER!

These happy companions play together for hours. Sometimes Bambi follows his rabbit friend, and sometimes Ben hops along in the lead.

PRUDENCE & HENRY

Prudence the pig was born very small. As with many stories about helpless young pigs, her future did not look bright. But that all changed when, at five weeks old, Prudence was taken to the Wildlives animal sanctuary. There she instantly befriended a family of puppies, and one of the puppies—Henry—became her best friend!

Henry started out bigger than Prudence. But after a month, Prudence was two times bigger than Henry—even though she acted as if they were the same size.

Prudence caught on quickly to Henry's games. They chase sticks together and bounce around playfully. It's possible Prudence thinks she's just one of the pups!

When it's time to sleep, Henry and Prudence curl up together. The rescue adopted Prudence so these two pals could remain together!

AOCHAN & GOHAN

At the Okoku Zoo, two animals have drawn many curious looks—a Japanese rat snake and a dwarf hamster. Aochan the snake and Gohan the hamster shared a cage for six years, ever since Gohan was given to Aochan for a meal. But instead of a meal, Gohan became Aochan's best friend!

Rat snakes usually like to eat rodents, but maybe Gohan didn't look very tasty, because Aochan's first instinct was to snuggle up to his hamster friend!

Gohan means "cooked rice" or "meal" in Japanese.

Aochan is 3 feet long and can wrap himself around his 3½-inch friend ten times. Gohan doesn't seem to notice. He's perfectly comfortable as Aochan watches over him.

Gohan enjoys napping buried in Aochan's coils. Aochan's cool, smooth back is the perfect resting place for his furry friend.

FRIENDS FOREVER!

JOCK & DAFFY

★ **CAMBRIDGE, ENGLAND** ★

Jock, a West Highland terrier, found an unexpected friend when his owner rescued eggs from an abandoned duck's nest. After two weeks of incubation in a cupboard, one little duckling hatched. She was named Daffy, and Jock took an instant liking to her.

Jock's owner received instructions from the Wildlife Society on how to incubate the duck eggs.

Jock protects his feathered friend, waiting for Daffy every morning before heading outside. Jock and Daffy like to run around and chase each other.

Baby ducks, or ducklings, will imprint on the first large animal or object they see. This means they behave like that creature or thing.

Daffy imprinted on Jock—she follows him everywhere and makes a squawking ruckus when he's out of sight.

FRIENDS 4EVER

MACAQUE & KITTEN

☆ BALI, INDONESIA ☆

At the Monkey Forest Park in the Ubud region of Bali, a sweet and unusual animal pair can often be seen cuddling—a wild long-tailed macaque (*muh-kak*) monkey and a ginger-colored kitten. After finding the kitten stumbling around the forest, the macaque picked her up and let her sleep in his lap. The two became inseparable.

The macaque is very protective of the kitten, shielding her when other monkeys come near. He has even been known to cover the kitten with a leaf so others won't bother her.

The macaque and the kitten take walks to explore the thick forest, or just sit and enjoy each other's company.

The macaque grooms the kitten as a mother might. The fluffy ginger-colored kitten enjoys the affection.

BALOO, SHERE KHAN & LEO

☆ LOCUST GROVE, GEORGIA ☆

Eleven years ago, the most unlikely trio of cubs was rescued in Atlanta—Baloo the bear, Shere Khan the tiger, and Leo the lion. The cubs were all two months old when they were taken to Noah's Ark zoo. Because the three had been living together like siblings, the zookeepers decided not to separate them. Instead, they built a habitat just for this special family.

The three have grown up—Shere Khan and Leo are both about 350 pounds, and Baloo weighs almost 1,000 pounds! They all live together in their own clubhouse, with lots of grass and a creek nearby to play in.

Leo is the early riser, awake every morning before the others. But once all are awake, the three wrestle and play until dinnertime. Baloo likes to give his giant tiger friend a real-life bear hug. Shere Khan loves to cuddle with Baloo.

Not only do these three play and eat together; they pile up for warmth and comfort when it's time to sleep.

In the wild, Bengal tigers usually live alone, but Shere Khan is happy in his family of three.

CHARLIE & KOSTYA

☆ NEW SOUTH WALES, AUSTRALIA ☆

In the village of North Star, a six-week-old wild piglet named Charlie found his way into a field with two huge bulls named Kostya and Blackie. Many people thought the bulls would run him off, but they seemed to like the wild piglet.

Charlie follows Kostya as he roams the farm. But with his little legs, Charlie must run to keep up with the large bull. He is barely as tall as Kostya's hoof!

Kostya weighs more than 2,000 pounds, and Charlie weighs less than 20!

As Kostya wanders the farm grazing or eating grass, Charlie follows his lead and enjoys a snack, too!

BFF

When Kostya tires of grazing and lies down for a rest, Charlie nestles into the giant bull to keep warm. Kostya never seems to mind the extra company.

BROCK & BUMBLEBEE

☆ SOMERSET, ENGLAND ☆

The Secret World Wildlife Rescue was home to two small furry pals. Brock the otter and Bumblebee the badger met when they were orphaned and taken to the center as babies. They developed a special friendship while exploring and playing together.

BFF

Brock and Bumblebee are about the same size—and both are low to the ground—which makes tumbling together in the grass so much fun.

Brock sometimes rides around (or tries to ride) on Bumblebee's back just as he would ride on his mother in the wild.

Most badgers in the wild prefer solitude, but after a day of playing, Bumblebee snuggles up with Brock to rest.

ZINZI & BOB

★ SUN CITY, SOUTH AFRICA ★

The Predator World zoo covers almost 2,500 acres and houses 36 species, including lions, tigers, cheetahs, leopards, reptiles, and birds. Among those animals were Zinzi the lioness cub and Bob the meerkat. Zinzi was brought to the zoo as a newborn after she was abandoned. There she met Bob, a two-year-old meerkat kept by the zoo's owner.

When they first met, Bob began following Zinzi around. It didn't take long for these two to become inseparable.

Zinzi and Bob eat their meals together and even go to the watering hole together. After a day of play, they lounge around and enjoy the warm South African sun.

A meerkat weighs an average of less than 2 pounds. A full-grown lioness can weigh between 265 and 400 pounds!

Bob loves to cuddle, and Zinzi's huge paw makes a cozy blanket as he burrows into her soft fur.

ROCKY & CINDY

☆ **SOMERSET, ENGLAND** ☆

The unlikely friendship of Rocky the Great Dane and Cindy the roe deer fawn began when Cindy was brought to the Secret World Wildlife Rescue. Cindy was just days old, and Rocky, owned by one of the center's employees, took Cindy under his protection.

These two pals like to take walks together. Rocky wanders slowly as Cindy follows close behind or next to him.

Whenever Cindy is feeling nervous or startled, Rocky rushes to her side. Rocky nuzzles the little fawn affectionately, as if she were one of his own puppies.

BFF

Rocky weighs 126 pounds. A two-week-old fawn weighs only about 12–15 pounds.

Cindy can often be found cuddled against Rocky, who sits tall and alert—ready to protect his friend.

BELLA & MAGGIE

☆ **ESSEX, ENGLAND** ☆

The fact that one was trained to hunt the other doesn't seem to matter to these two friends. Maggie the fox was found on the side of the road, unable to hunt for her own food. Her best friend, Bella the foxhound, was separated from her hunting pack and left behind. After both were taken to the Wildlives animal sanctuary, they met and have since found happiness hanging out together!

Instead of chasing foxes like Maggie—as Bella was trained to do—she walks alongside her friend, enjoying the company.

Maggie takes care of other fox cubs at the sanctuary, but it's Bella who looks after Maggie. Bella stands firm and protective, while Maggie sometimes cuddles up safely beneath her.

CUTE BFFs

Bella and Maggie enjoy running around and playing on the grounds.

OMNI & DIGBY

☆ LAIKIPIA, KENYA ☆

In 2000, a baby black rhinoceros named Omni was rescued from his mother, who was unable to care for him. He was brought to the Lewa Wildlife Conservancy when he was just four weeks old. There he met Digby, an orphaned warthog.

Warthogs are wild pigs that live in Africa.

In the wild, birds and his mother would help keep Omni free of ticks and flies. Instead, Digby steps in! He roots around and eats the bugs to help Omni stay clean.

BFF

To cool off from the hot African sun, Omni and Digby roll in the mud together. After playing, Omni sometimes rests his heavy head on Digby's back.

Omni and Digby also sleep together—often with Digby lying on top of Omni. They keep each other warm and comfortable.

The African black rhinoceros is classified as "critically endangered," which means the number of black rhinoceroses in the world is rapidly decreasing.

PADDLE POP & ANGUS

☆ MELBOURNE, AUSTRALIA ☆

When Paddle Pop, an abandoned Maltese mix, was adopted, she gained not only a new home, but also a new friend—Angus the green-cheeked parakeet. Angus was known to have a bad temper, but Paddle Pop's gentle nature calmed him.

 Angus likes to keep Paddle Pop well groomed—he often nips and plucks Paddle Pop's soft, curly hair!

Angus is happy when he rides around on Paddle Pop's back—and Paddle Pop likes to play along.

Green-cheeked parakeets are smart, and Angus is no exception. He has taught himself to bark! Angus likes to bark and whistle to get Paddle Pop's attention.

sWEET Friends

REX & REX JR.

⭐ VICTORIA, AUSTRALIA ⭐

One day, while out with his owner, a wirehaired pointing griffon named Rex passed a kangaroo that had been hit by a car. Rex sensed there was something wrong. He went to the kangaroo and gently pulled a baby from its pouch. Rex carefully carried the little joey back to his owner. Rex and the joey bonded immediately. The joey was named Rex Jr. in honor of the friend that saved him.

A baby kangaroo is called a joey!

Rex and Rex Jr. play together in the grass. Even though he's much tinier than Rex, little Rex Jr. uses his strong legs to keep up with his friend.

♥ BEST ♥
BUDDIES

Rex Jr. likes to snuggle against Rex. Rex sniffs and licks the little kangaroo.

THEMBA & ALBERT

☆ EASTERN CAPE, SOUTH AFRICA ☆

The Shamwari Game Reserve became home to Themba and Albert. When he was just six months old, Themba, an orphaned elephant, was rescued and taken to the reserve, where he met Albert the sheep. Albert turned out to be just the friend he needed!

Themba chased after Albert the first time they met. Albert, of course, ran away to hide. When Albert finally came out, Themba kept sniffing him with his trunk. He was curious about his new woolly friend.

forever friends!

Albert likes to do what Themba does. He even learned how to eat from an acacia bush by watching Themba carefully work around the thorns.

These two can be seen by each other's side all over the reserve.

Themba and Albert explore the bush together for hours. When it's time to rest, they lounge and cuddle up next to each other. Themba sometimes rests his trunk on Albert's soft back.

ZOYA & FRIDA

Dogs love to chase cats, and at the Warsaw Zoo, it's no different. Frida, a long-haired German shepherd puppy, loves to chase Zoya, a Sumatran tiger. Zoya was abandoned and brought to the zoo when she was just three months old. There she was introduced to Frida, who was also three months old. They became instant companions—and now they are all grown up!

Sumatran tigers are an endangered species. Zoya is part of the European Endangered Species Programme (EEP).

When Frida was still a puppy, she would chase her best friend, Zoya. After a few years, Zoya could run almost ten miles per hour faster than her canine friend—but Zoya would slow down sometimes so Frida could catch her!

By the time Zoya was a few years old, she weighed almost four times more than Frida! But that didn't stop their play. Zoya lets Frida step over her and roll her over on her back while they wrestle.

When done chasing each other and wrestling, the pals nuzzle and rest.

BFF

BILLY & LILLY

★ BUCKFASTLEIGH, ENGLAND ★

Billy the boxer looked out for his pal Lilly the kid. When Lilly was born, she was the smallest kid in the litter. Her mother could care only for her two stronger siblings, so Billy stepped in and began watching over the tiny goat when she was just twelve days old.

Baby goats are called kids.

Male dogs rarely nurture or adopt even a puppy, but that is not true of Billy. He looks after Lilly, often putting a paw or a leg around her. Lilly snuggles into her big boxer buddy.

After Lilly eats, Billy knows how to clean her up! Lilly can count on Billy to be there for her.

These two race through Pennywell Farm & Wildlife Centre, playing together. And when they tire, they snuggle up together and sleep.

TIMON & PUMBAA

★ WORCESTERSHIRE, ENGLAND ★

When Timon the meerkat saw Pumbaa the micro pig through the fence in a neighboring pen, he tried hard to get to him. The two were born just a few weeks apart, and once they met, the folks at Tropical Inc education center couldn't keep them apart. Timon and Pumbaa were moved into a pen together!

Like their namesakes in *The Lion King*, Timon and Pumbaa are young and carefree. Timon is outgoing, and Pumbaa is more reserved—but together they make a great pair!

A newborn micro pig is small enough to fit in a teacup!

These two fuzzy friends are about the same size, and they spend entire days having fun just being together.

SWEET Friends

EVEN MORE ANIMAL BFFs

CHINO & FALSTAFF
★ MEDFORD, OREGON ★

Some friendships seem impossible, but this pair proves that friends can turn up anywhere! Chino, a golden retriever, and Falstaff, a 15-inch koi, met when Chino spotted Falstaff in the backyard pond. Chino would peer into the water to watch Falstaff swim around. Falstaff would appear every time, greeting Chino, who would happily wag his tail.

GRACE & MINTY
★ DEVON, ENGLAND ★

A foal is a young horse.

While being treated for an injured leg, Grace the racing foal found an unexpected friend in Minty the black lamb. Minty stayed by Grace's side as she recovered. The two then played and ate together during the day, and curled up in the hay together at night.